# When A Man
# Faces Grief

## Additional Books by the Authors

### Thomas R. Golden

*Swallowed by a Snake*

■

### James E. Miller

*What Will Help Me? / How Can I Help?*
*When You're Ill or Incapacitated / When You're the Caregiver*
*How Will I Get Through the Holidays?*
*One You Love Is Dying*
*When You Know You're Dying*
*Winter Grief, Summer Grace*
*Autumn Wisdom*
*The Caregiver's Book*
*Welcoming Change*
*A Pilgrimage Through Grief*
*Helping the Bereaved Celebrate the Holidays*
*A Little Book for Preachers*
*Effective Support Groups*
*The Rewarding Practice of Journal Writing*

■

# When A Man
# Faces Grief

## 12 Practical Ideas to Help You
## Heal from Loss

Thomas R. Golden

and

James E. Miller

Willowgreen Publishing

*To Whitten (1981-1998) and his father Carlton.*

We are indebted to a number of people who have assisted in a number of ways in the editing of this book. They include Helen Wadsworth, John Peterson, Bernie Miller, Jennifer Levine, John Ladd, James Jones, Carrie Hackney, Miles Goldstein, Darbie Golden, Chris Crawford, Clare Barton, and Michael Abrahams.

Willowgreen Publishing
PO Box 25180
Fort Wayne, Indiana 46825
219/424-7916

Library of Congress Catalogue
Card Number: 98-90047

ISBN 1-885933-27-4

This book focuses on the *masculine side* of healing from loss. This masculine side covers only a part of the multitude of ways there are to heal. In reality, there are as many ways to heal as there are people who are healing. Unfortunately, our culture tends to embrace and acknowledge only a small portion of these many ways. Often the types of healing our culture endorses are what are considered the traditionally feminine ways which are characterized by talking about the loss, by crying, and by sharing one's emotions with others. While these are very good ways to heal, they are not the *only* ways. We believe that masculine grievers have been too often misunderstood and unfairly judged simply because their approach has not been as commonly understood or accepted.

This book will begin to bring some light to these ways and offer you many ideas about these masculine paths. We fully expect that you, both men and women, are already using the various types of healing that you are about to read. Most likely, it comes naturally to you. We hope that in reading this book you can affirm and strengthen the healing that you are already doing.

The purpose of any healing mode, masculine or feminine, is to give people a *safe* way to connect with their grief and pain. Many people find that the more commonly accepted feminine mode of talking about their pain with their family and friends provides a safe way to do this. This feminine mode is well known. It's characterized by emphasizing *interaction* with intimate others, expressing the emotions on a verbal level, talking about the past, and emoting freely. On the other hand, many men  and those who grieve in the masculine style often don't find talking about their grief as a particularly safe thing to do. For a variety of reasons they find safety elsewhere. That's an important subject we address in this book.

In these pages you will read how this masculine side tends to prefer to connect with the grief through *action* rather than interaction. The masculine side prefers to heal by changing the future rather than talking about the past. It usually uses fewer words and because of this, it is often less visible. These differences and others make the masculine side a quieter and more subtle form of healing. Don't be fooled by its quietness though. It is still a very powerful way to heal.

We want to be clear that the masculine side of healing is used by both men and women. It would be a mistake to say that all men heal in one way and all women another. This is simply not so. The truth is that we all use both sides. Women will use the masculine side in their healing just as many men will find the feminine ways helpful. It is how we blend the masculine and the feminine sides that makes us unique. As people we are too complex to be put into boxes. Importantly, there are men who will choose the feminine mode as a pre-dominant way of healing and this is fine. We need to use caution when it comes to judging anyone about the way they choose to heal.

This book is comprised of twelve short chapters, each offering practical help in negotiating the tough terrain of grief. It offers valuable information to help you get oriented amid the chaos that usually accompanies this difficult time. We hope you will find it written in a male friendly manner and, more than that, that you find it both insightful and helpful. Please know that there is a great deal of information in the "other side" of this book that you will find useful in your healing too. We encourage you to read what is being offered to those who want to support you and people like you.

You'll find twelve short, easy-to-read chapters here. They're designed to introduce you to the basics of masculine grief and to help you identify your own path through grief without forcing you to spend undue time in this learning process. We'll be making these major points:

- Start where you are.
- Learn the terrain.
- Determine your strength.
- Approach your grief by way of your strength.
- Tap into your grief with actions and rituals.
- Monitor your progress by using a map.
- Care for those around you.
- Take good care of yourself.
- Tell your story.
- Call upon your courage.
- Open yourself to that which is deepest and highest.
- Build on this experience and use it for all it's worth.

Tom Golden
Jim Miller

# 1
## Start where you are.

This may seem like a simple step, but it's an important one: you must begin with what has happened to you. Whatever has occurred in your life, you have lost something, or maybe *many* things. Whatever you have lost, that's what you start with.

Perhaps someone close to you has died. Maybe it was your spouse or lover, your child or grandchild, your parent or sibling, and your life feels as if it has been turned upside down. Maybe it's a good friend or a close colleague who is now gone, and while that person may not have been central in your life, still you feel their absence.

Perhaps you find yourself single again after an important relationship has ended. It matters not whether this breakup was expected or unexpected, whether it was your own choice or the decision was made for you—the sense of loss is still present. If you're now separated or divorced or widowed, you may be experiencing other losses as well—the possible loss of your home, for example, or the loss of your friends, your familiar routine, your sexual partner, your sense of security.

Maybe you've changed jobs or entered another career and you've left behind a certain level of comfort or stability, including the network of friends you developed or the sense of competence you experienced through your work. If you were forced to make this move against your will, the loss may seem ever greater. The same can be true if you've recently retired, whether you wanted to or not. You'll know a still different kind of loss if you're *between* jobs and you're not sure what the future holds.

You may have lost your health, either temporarily or permanently. An accident, illness, or disability may be changing the way you live your life for a long time, and perhaps forever. A serious financial reversal or some other personal mishap can be affecting you in a similar way. Coming to grips with an addiction always carries with it a sense of loss too.

Whatever has happened, you're now without something you used to have or you're missing someone who's been a part of your life. Where once there was a presence, now there's an absence. Where once there was a completeness, now there's a hole. While it's not pleasant to face these losses, in the long run that's still the best thing to do—face them. It's unwise to ignore such events or pretend they didn't happen.

Depending on the losses you've experienced, it may be hard for you to take it all in. It may even seem impossible to do that. This will all take time. But the only way for you to eventually accept what has happened and to make it a part of your life is to acknowledge the truth—the place you find yourself is not where you want to be. Something is missing, and you wish it weren't.

■

# 2

## Learn the terrain.

When you have suffered a loss, especially one you didn't want or expect, chances are good you'll find yourself in unfamiliar territory. Even if you saw this change coming, or even if you had some control over what happened, this can still be a strange experience that takes some getting used to. Things are not the way they were before.

A word many men use for their experience of loss is "chaos." What used to be dependable and orderly becomes unpredictable and confusing. It's a disturbing time. You're likely to feel ill-at-ease. Your stomach may get upset. Your head may ache. You may be "up" one minute and "down" the next and not have a clue as to how this happens, or why. You may become depressed, perhaps more than you ever have. You may get angrier than normal, either at other people or at yourself. You may blow up at little things in ways that surprise or embarrass you.

Some men tend to feel guilty at times like this. They recall things they've done that they wish they hadn't, or they stew over what they wish they *had* done but didn't. Perhaps you're like that now. Some men carry a sense of fear for what may yet happen. Some feel awkward and ashamed, wondering how they appear to others and what those others are thinking about them.

On the other hand, you may go about your days unaware you're feeling much at all. When someone asks, you may act as if nothing has happened. You may do that because you think that's what a man is supposed to do, or because it feels right for you at the moment, or because you're not sure what else to do.

One of the most helpful things you can do early in your grief is the same thing you can do when you're walking or driving through an area where you haven't been before. You can pay close attention to what you're passing by so you'll know if you begin to re-trace your steps, or so you can find your way back if you need to. You can leave markers behind as you walk, or make mental notes as you drive. By doing these things you get to know the terrain.

You can do something similar as you enter the territory of loss and grief. You can pay particular attention to what's around you and within you as you travel here. You can take note of the scenes you see, the turns you take, the general direction you're heading. You can draw upon what you've learned through the years. You can ask yourself questions: What is this time like? What does it compare to? What does it have in common with other difficult experiences I've lived through? What's predictable about it? What's unpredictable?

Examine in some detail this territory you're in. Is your loss temporary or permanent, or do you know yet? Is it an unfortunate hindrance or a severe handicap? Is it a challenge you're prepared to overcome, or does it threaten to overcome you? Where does your hope lie?

Survey your surroundings. Who has remained with you and who has joined you? Whom or what can you count on? Where are the dangers? Where are your safe places?

Spend some time figuring out what you've lost and what you're leaving behind. But also be clear about what you still have left, about what you have going for you. Sometimes talking it over with another person can help; they may be able to see what you cannot at the moment. All men are different in the way they learn their terrain. Some men write things down. Others mull things over as they jog or walk, as they weed gardens or read books.

In the ways that work best for you, get acquainted with this place where you find yourself, because whether you like it or not, you're going to be here for a little while. And the better you get your bearings today, the better you'll be able to find your way tomorrow.

■

# 3
## Determine your strength.

A time of serious loss can be a very trying experience. What used to give you joy or satisfaction now leaves you with sadness or emptiness. What used to provide significance to your life may now threaten to rob it of meaning.

You're learning the difficult truth that grief is hard work. It depletes your energy and saps your spirit. It reduces your ability to concentrate. It gets in the way of your capacity to make decisions. Grief often lasts much longer than you expect. It sometimes demands of you more than you think you have to give.

With all these reasons to dislike grief, what is the best way to deal with it? This way: by letting it into your life. Why? Because grief has an important purpose. It helps you heal. It allows you, in time, to feel better. It shows you how you can grow from your loss rather than just be diminished by it. The fact is, it's only by grieving that you can heal. If in one way or another you do not grieve, you will not move forward.

So go ahead: experience it. Allow your grief to do its work, bit by bit, pang by pang, perhaps even tear by tear. Each time you grieve a little, you move ahead a little. Each time you step toward your grief, you step closer to your healing.

What is the best way for you as a man to make your way there? Usually, by way of your strength. You are normally more sure of yourself when you're doing what you know you do well. Common sense advises you to turn to your strongest ally when you're in trouble. In grief you can use your strength as this ally to connect with your pain so it can diminish a little at a time.

Figure out what your natural strengths are. Be aware of the skills you've acquired. Know where your power resides. To do that, ask yourself questions like these:

- *What am I good at?*
- *What do I look forward to doing?*

■ *What has become second nature to me, so I do it without even thinking?*

■ *What gives me a deep sense of pride?*

■ *What has brought me success in the past?*

■ *What are the positives others see in me?*

Your strength may turn out to be your thinking ability— the way you sort things out logically and analyze them objectively. Or it may be your tendency to stay more with your emotions in your day-to-day living, making you more demonstrative in your approach to life and other people. You may be inclined to concentrate on what's tangible—what can be seen and heard, touched and handled. Or you may prefer to rely more on the intangible, things like your imagination, your intuition, and your artistic sense. You may be an extrovert by nature, ready to be around and to converse with other people. Or you may be an introvert, preferring your solitude and the inner world of your own thoughts and impressions. You may be the type who wants things well planned and carefully ordered. Or you may be one who's likely to be flexible and spontaneous, prepared to follow your whims, even at a time like this.

Whatever you are like, and whatever you like to do, know where your strengths lie. The better you understand them and the more you appreciate them, the more easily you can be ready to have them at your disposal.

■

# 4

## Approach your grief by way of your strength.

No one has ever suffered the very same loss you have. If someone else's partner or child or parent has died, just as yours has, that loss is not the same as yours. Even if two of you are mourning the death of the same family member, you each have had your own history and relationship with that person, your own memories to recall and your own issues to work through. Similarly, no one else's divorce or job loss or physical disability could ever be mistaken for yours.

Just as your loss is original, *you* are original too. No one has ever had your same experiences, your same make-up, your same hopes and dreams. Nor has anyone ever had your exact assortment of strengths and abilities. Those unique traits of yours can give you an edge in facing what lies before you. In a time that seems uncertain, you will do well to fall back upon what you know with certainty. Your strengths have served you well before. Let them serve you well now by helping you consciously connect with your pain a piece at a time as you slowly whittle away at your grief.

Do you like being active? Then move around, use your body, tackle a project, help out others. One man found a path to grieve his brother's suicide by training hard for a tennis tournament each of them had wanted to win. Every time he practiced, he was with both his brother and his pain. He found a way to connect his action with his grief and, yes, after three years of staying at it, he won the tournament.

Are you good with your mind? Then use it. Think your way through what's happening, what you want to do. Come up with goals that are clear and plans that are workable. One man who lost his job through corporate downsizing started by reading all he could about how to deal with major life transitions. Then he enrolled in a course on the subject. Next thing he knew, he was helping others with his knowledge. Today that's become his business.

Are you a people person? Then place yourself among those with whom you can talk and listen, and find ways you can share in other ways too. A man whose wife died after forty years of marriage became a volunteer in the hospital where she had been cared for. Another man chose to visit new patients in a rehabilitation center after he became a paraplegic in an auto accident. Each was using his activity to connect with and work through his grief.

Are you best at doing things with your hands? Then do *more* things with your hands and use that experience to reflect upon what has happened to you. A widower who was a wood-worker used his skills to create blocks and toys for the nursery school where his wife had taught. Each time he gave his creations away, he explained why he had chosen to do what he did. And each time he tapped into his grief a little more.

Are you a quiet one? Then write rather than talk if that feels right. Or take slow walks. Or listen to soothing music. Or just sit in silence and reflect. Are you expressive emotionally? Then cry or laugh, rant or rave, show your astonishment or display your love. Are you precise by nature? Then try keeping track of your grief with a daily record of what is happening inside, including the progress you make. Are you impulsive? Then improvise as you go along. Down-to-earth? Then do what seems most practical.

In the various ways that seem right for you, call upon your God-given strengths to lead you into and through your time of grief. Tap into your pain by using those skills that seem most natural to you. Remember that each time you do that, you move yourself that much closer to your healing.

■

# 5

## Tap into your grief with actions and rituals.

Grief is not just something that comes at you and overtakes you, like an outsider elbowing its way into your life. It comes just as much from *inside* you. It's an inward response growing out of what's been very important in your life. While it may not always seem this way, you can have an influence on your grief at the same time it is having its influence on you.

By giving yourself meaningful ways to deal internally and externally with what has changed in your life, you create valuable opportunities to help yourself heal. By chipping away at your grief, you gradually give release to the pain that lies within and you gradually prepare yourself for what will come next in your life. One effective way of doing this involves rituals.

A ritual is simply an action you consciously take that gives you a way to remember your loss as you connect with the emotions that flow from that loss. A ritual is a tool that allows you to linger in that association for a few moments and to feel safe as you do so, knowing that your ritual will shortly lead you back to everyday life. It's a contained space you create in which you can temporarily let yourself go and give yourself freedom to grieve. If you'd like examples of this, read back through the activities described in the previous chapter— those are all rituals.

Rituals need not be elaborate ceremonies. They can be quite short, quite simple. Or they may take much longer. They can be performed when you're alone or when you're with others. Just as saying grace can be a ritual that begins a meal, and singing the national anthem can be a ritual that starts a sporting event, you can use rituals to guide you toward re-membering what has happened and toward connecting with the emotions you carry. Men commonly use three kinds of grief rituals.

■ *Rituals of Thought.* At its simplest, a ritual of thought might involve pausing to admire a photograph or to hold a special memento that is associated with what you have lost. Lighting a candle, honoring a significant date, or re-visiting a meaningful site are other examples. You might leaf through a scrapbook, watch a homemade video, or listen to a song that carries special memories. Meditation can be a ritual. So can writing a letter to whoever or whatever is now gone.

■ *Rituals of Practicality.* These actions add another element to conscious remembrance: tangible usefulness. After a loved one has died, you might arrange a fitting memorial, including perhaps a "living memorial"—a gift that serves others or an action that promotes an interest of the one who is gone. As a result of your loss, you might become a teacher or guide or companion to others. You might dedicate your life work to some higher purpose. You could make constructive changes in your own life as a conscious tribute to what has happened to you.

■ *Rituals of Creativity.* The added dimension here is that your creative urges and instincts are channeled into your actions. You might draw or paint a response to your loss. You might sculpt a figure in clay or carve an object in wood. You could write a poem or a book, compose a song or a talk, or express yourself with a musical instrument, a whittling knife, or a box of tools.

These are all means of moving *toward* your grief so you can move *through* your grief. And while you look forward to a time when you can feel better again, you can often experience something rather surprising right in the middle of the rituals you create. There is a simple beauty and a quiet comfort to those times that helps you feel a little better already.

■

# 6

## Monitor your progress by using a map.

Adjusting to loss can be a very slow process. Taking the rollercoaster ride through grief can be an unsettling experience. Sometimes you may wonder how anything more could happen to you. At other times you may wonder if anything is happening at all—everything seems to be at a standstill. Understanding the process of grief, or having a road map for it, will help you.

Remember: everyone grieves in different ways and for different lengths of time. Moreover, some griefs pass more quickly than others—usually the less serious ones, or the ones you anticipate and prepare for. Other griefs may last a long, long time. A few griefs, in fact, may never completely go away; you learn to live with them. But most grief follows a general pattern, whether it naturally lasts days or months or years.

■ A *time of disbelief.* Often when the loss first occurs, and almost always when the loss is unexpected, you're in shock for awhile. The whole experience seems confusing and unreal. You think, "This cannot be so!" But it is.

■ A *time of pain.* As the protective shock wears off, the hurt sets in. Many emotions may wash over you. Often the strongest ones for men are sadness, loneliness, helplessness, guilt, and anger. Your anger may seem overpowering and all-consuming. You may be mad at whoever or whatever caused this loss, or at the loss itself, or at yourself, or at God. You may yearn for life to return to the way it once was. You may be unusually forgetful, or uncharacteristically tired, or uncommonly stressed. You may even feel a little crazy—many grieving people do.

■ A *time of growing acceptance.* If grief were compared to the seasons of the year, this would be winter. Time slows or even stops. Life grows quieter. You may feel listless and useless, discouraged or depressed. You may think a lot about the past and have serious questions about the future. Most men feel not much is going on during this time, but actually a lot is happening within. You're letting go of what used to be so you can make room for what is yet to come.

■ *A time of re-awakened potential.* This is the springtime of your grief. Your energy and interests begin to return. You assume more control of your life in bits and pieces. You learn to forgive some things and forget others. You begin to find ways to make your loss a part of you rather than apart from you. You begin to hope again. You're still sad at times, but you can sense that you've turned a corner somehow.

■ *A time of renewed life.* Eventually, by alternately working with your grief and surrendering to it, you will be led back to life. You will not be the same person you were before, for you will have changed and grown. If your loss was the death of a loved one, you can begin to develop a new kind of relationship with that person—a relationship that transcends time. If your loss took another form, then you can begin to live your life in ways that take into account what you have been through and what you have learned as a result.

This entire process is very fluid. You'll move both forward and backward through these periods. Sometimes you may feel as if you're stuck and you're not going anywhere at all. That happens to many people. By making your way resolutely through your grief, and by going where your grief leads you, you'll find upon looking back that you've been following a path. While that trail may weave, it still has its direction. While the way ahead is sometimes unclear, your journey still has a purpose. You may feel that you've only been wandering, but in retrospect you'll see that you've been finding your way home.

■

# 7

## Care for those around you.

It's likely you're inclined to be a provider. Most men are.
You want to meet the needs of those in your care. You're
ready to guard and protect, to shelter and support, to nurture.
This tendency has been bred into you culturally, socially, and
biologically. Because it's such an integral part of you, you dare
not ignore it. Still, there's an additional reason for you to
honor this instinctive behavior. Your acts of caring for others
can be an important pathway through your own grief.

When you reach out to hold and help those who are close
to you and counting on you, you can also be helping yourself
at the same time. Why is that? Because when you consciously
allow your caring for others to be a link to your own pain, you
encourage the natural unfolding of your own grief. And that's
directly related to the natural advance of your own healing.

Here are some examples of how you can care for others and
promote your own return to life at the same time:

■ *Accept others' unique ways of grieving.* Many factors have
influenced how others do their mourning, just as has been the
case with you. When you encourage them to grieve in the
ways that best suit them, even if that's different than your way,
that gives you greater freedom too. You may also find that
their expressions of loss can help you get more in touch with
what's going on inside you. The tears of others, for example,
can sometimes clear the way for your own.

■ *Open the doors of communication.* When you allow others
to say whatever is on their minds and hearts, even if it's not
what you're experiencing, you pave the way for greater understanding. It's good if you can listen as fully as you're able,
knowing that it usually helps when people unburden themselves in this way. This can become a pathway for you to tap
into your own reactions too, either as they're talking to you or
as you respond to them. Remember that a look, a touch, or

even a silence can sometimes communicate as much as any number of words.

■ *Accept your helplessness.* No one likes to feel powerless. That's doubly true for those who see themselves as strong and independent. If that's part of how you operate, this can be a trying time for you. People who are protectors don't like it when they cannot protect. The reality is, however, that it's not in your power to take away another's pain. And even if you could, you *shouldn't.* Then the other would not do what she or he alone must do in order to learn and grow from this loss. Of course, there's a lesson waiting for you here too.

■ *Care for your loved ones' ordinary needs.* Sometimes the best way to care for people's emotional needs is simply to care for their basic physical needs. When you do things like prepare a special meal, wash another's car, give a backrub, send flowers, or read a favorite bedtime story, you're showing in quiet ways that you remember what's happened to them. More than that, these can equally be ways that you remember what's happened to you.

■ *Allow others to care for you too.* Keep in mind that other people often want and need to provide care, just as you do. And don't forget that you deserve care, just as others do. In accepting the care of others, you by your example give permission for everyone to accept that nurturing that can come from those around.

■ *Remember that you may be quite limited in the care you can provide.* Your resources may be at an all-time low. You may not be able to care for those you love as much as you're accustomed. If that's the case, go easy on yourself. Accept your limits. Your former energies will return in time.

In the meantime, simply allow your acts of caring to be connection points with your sense of loss and your own experience of grief. It doesn't matter whether that connection is seen by others or not. What matters is that you see it and know it yourself.

■

# 8

## Take good care of yourself.

You cannot care for others if you do not give good care to yourself. Otherwise you'll have nothing to give. Even apart from helping others, it's important to take care of yourself for your *own* sake. A time of serious loss is a time of personal depletion. Your mind may work overtime and lose its edge. Your spirit may drag. Your body can react to the stress of all that's happening, whether you realize it or not. Of all times of your life, this is a period when it's especially right to care for your own needs.

■ *Care for your physical needs.* It's easy to forgo your normal routines when so many demands press upon you. Yet this is precisely when certain life-giving habits of yours can become literally life-saving. What you eat, how much you eat, and the way you eat directly affect your physical and mental fitness. So eat regularly, moderately, and wisely. Drink plenty of water. Monitor carefully the intake of any alcohol and other self-medications. Pace yourself throughout the day and do what you can to get the rest you need, both during the day and at night. Make sure you exercise at least three or four times a week. Arrange for a physical exam with your doctor if you haven't had one recently.

■ *Care for your emotional needs.* You have emotional needs as much as the next person, but you may have learned to downplay or hide them. As you're aware, that's what our culture often expects men to do. When strong emotions of grief arise, do you find ways to let them flow? You'll hasten your own healing if you find ways to express what is building inside you. Contrary to what you were told, grown men *do* cry at times. And that's okay! You can also do any number of other things to care for yourself emotionally. You can take the initiative to confide in family members or friends, counselors or clergy. You may join a group or attend a workshop or seminar on dealing with loss. You may keep a journal or jog. You may engage in vigorous outdoor activity—hiking through the woods, photographing in the great outdoors, or gardening up a storm—aware all the while that what you're doing is taking care of yourself.

■ *Care for your social needs.* Loss can disrupt existing relationships. Friends may drop away, temporarily or permanently, when death comes or divorce occurs. Colleagues disappear when jobs end. People who have been close may not know what to say or do when tragedy strikes or illness hits. Consequently, they may stay away and do nothing. It's worth noting that grieving people often desire more time alone. Solitude can calm and replenish you. But rare is the man who wishes to be completely alone. You can satisfy your social needs by reaching out to those you want to be around, and by responding to those who reach out to you. You can seek new relationships. You can seek out those leisure and professional activities that provide the human interaction you want.

■ *Care for your spiritual needs.* When your inner or outer life is in a state of flux, you may search for stability in other ways. You may wish to ground yourself in the comfort and inspiration your faith can provide. You may find support in congregational activities. You may find meaning in spiritual connection through quietness or in prayer, by reading scriptures or by talking with a spiritual director, or in any other way that feels appropriate and comfortable to you.

You deserve the best care possible. More than that, it may just be that you're the best one to provide it.

■

# 9

## Tell your story.

Every loss, and that includes *your* loss, is about much more than the facts of what once happened. Each loss also involves a story, a tale. That story deserves to be told, for several reasons.

■ *By telling the tale, you make it more real.* Sometimes it's hard to believe the loss you've experienced really happened or that it happened the way it did, especially if it was sudden or unexpected. Even if you had time to prepare yourself, your loss may have been too large for you to take in all at once. So you do it piecemeal, a little at a time. One way you can do that is by telling your story. Each time you weave a little more of the tale, whether it's to the same person or different people, you ease yourself toward accepting the hard truth: "Yes, this *is* real. Yes, it *did* happen."

■ *By telling the tale, you gain perspective.* Every loss, just like every story, has a beginning, a middle, and an end. Each part relates to the other and all parts relate to the whole. Sometimes you don't make those connections until you look at it all more closely. Interestingly enough, one way to look more closely is to stand back and look from farther away. Then you can see what happened in its totality. That's what you do as you weave your tale—you make it appear more complete, more whole. You can see themes and patterns you weren't able to see because you were in the middle of them. Whatever you see now, you can use it to help you live your life from here on out.

■ *By telling the tale, you gain witnesses.* It's one thing to experience your loss by yourself, learning as you go. It's another to have someone else witness what has happened and is happening to you. Witnesses help give weight and meaning to your experiences. They help validate your situation in life and confirm your outlook or your emotions. And whenever you have witnesses, you can also have companions—people who are able to stand with you when you need them most.

■ *By telling the tale, you gain power.* When you begin to accept that the past is past and cannot be changed, you can also begin to see that the present and the future do not have to be controlled by what used to be. You can have a significant say in what happens from this point forward. More than *telling* your story, you can do much toward *creating* the *rest* of your story.

■ *In telling the tale, you can help others.* In the simple act of preserving a record of these events, you leave a legacy for others to remember. You leave lessons for people to absorb and by which they can direct their own lives. You can leave hope for those who will one day follow a similar path. In short, you can put your experience to the service of others.

So go ahead: weave your tale in the way that best suits you. If you're a writer, preserve it in a journal or a book, as musings or as poems, as biography or as history. Paint your story, or piece it together in photographs, or place it on videotape. However you choose to do it, tell your story.

■

# 10

## Call upon your courage.

Your courage is probably important to you. It is to most men. In all likelihood you absorbed the messages you were given as a boy: "Be strong." "Don't flinch." "Don't be a crybaby." It's likely you internalized the examples of determined, stoic manhood that came to you from all directions. You probably listened carefully when a male was described with approval as "the strong silent type."

These ideas about being strong and courageous may have served you well in the past. But the experience of serious loss has another truth to teach you: a man's grief sometimes requires a new understanding of what real courage is all about.

■ *Call on your courage to stay with your grief.* As you're learning, grief is a jumbled and disorderly affair. It creates havoc in your life. It's not the kind of experience you want to remain in for very long. Yet that's exactly what you're called upon to do—to find ways to experience your grief and not run from it, or hide from it, or pretend it's not there. This might also mean not dulling your pain with alcohol or various sorts of drugs, as well as not pushing to find a hasty replacement for your loss.

Your grief may require you to re-define what it means to be brave. Instead of acting unfazed, it may mean letting more of your emotions show. Instead of blocking tears, it may mean letting them fall. Instead of acting like nothing's the matter, it may mean going through your days aware that something *is* the matter—you're missing someone or something that's been very important to you. You must admit that truth and feel what it means for your life before you can heal.

■ *Call on your courage to stand in the tension.* Grief is unsettling. When the worst appears to be behind you, when you least expect it, wham!—grief hits you all over again. It can be

26

one of the most turbulent and disturbing life experiences you've ever known.

What's being asked of you is to find ways to remain in that tension, that uneasiness, for awhile and not expect your life to be otherwise for the time being. Depending on the nature of your loss, you may need to stay in the tension of your loneliness as you miss someone you've loved deeply, or to remain in the tension of your sadness as you miss something you've long cherished. You may be called upon to experience the tension of moving beyond your natural independence and allow yourself to depend on someone else for a change, which can feel very shaky if you're not used to it. Whatever form it takes, you're summoned to face the fluctuations and, for awhile at least, just let them be.

■ *Call on your courage to stand outside the circle.* When you allow yourself to grieve, you may act differently than you have in the past. You may appear to be outside the norm of what people have come to expect of men in general or of you in particular. It may take people a while to get used to this change in you. There's always a chance they will not get used to it at all. So this may be yet another way in which your courage will need to show itself—as you strive to be true to yourself as a grieving man, whatever others may think.

Robert Louis Stevenson, the Scottish writer who struggled daily with ill health until he died in early middle age, wrote, "Yours is no less noble because no drum beats when you go out to your daily battlefields, and no crowds shout when you return from your daily victory and defeat." The courage to grieve can be like that—a quiet, often unseen series of acts that is nothing less than heroic.

■

# 11

## Open yourself to that which is deepest and highest.

There is much to be learned from accumulated wisdom and modern research, from what others say and from what many do. It would be foolish to ignore all that knowledge and experience. Yet it would be equally foolish to *limit* yourself to that same base.

■ *There comes a time when you will do well to go where no one else can go: deep within.*

Richard of Saint-Victor, the great mystic, put it this way: "If you wish to search out the deep things of God, search out the depths of your own spirit." Here's another way of saying it: "Much of what you need to know is already located within you."

Every man who makes the journey to discover his own humanness will discover something more along the way. His inner essence is composed of another Essence. For no man is merely his own creation. He has been brought forth by more than his own parents. His body is fashioned out of something other than common chemical elements. His is a spark that is not his alone.

If you want to know that which is most true, go within. But go very deep within. If you want to discover what is most authentic, peel away those layers that cover you, one after another. But peel lovingly and carefully. If you want to be in touch with divine influence, direct your attention inward. Just give yourself lots of time and quiet.

■ *There comes a time for you to travel where no one else can travel for you: far beyond.*

Crushing loss and heavy grief can introduce you quite simply and directly to that other dimension in your life: the spiritual and the religious. In the midst of all that is mysterious around you, you may suddenly find yourself in the presence of The Mystery. As you struggle to fathom what is sweeping over you, you may come upon The Unfathomable. You may not have language to put to this experience, but that's okay—language isn't required. Words, in fact, may just get in your way.

You may find that this time has many of the natural makings of a spiritual pilgrimage. People who intentionally concentrate on their spiritual life often undertake disciplines that are similar to the ones that are now yours as you grieve: a time away from normal routines; increased silence around you; more aloneness; sometimes a darkness within your soul; revelations where you least expect them; gentle growth; deepening understanding.

■ *There will come a time for you to do what no one else can do for you: trust.*

Your life may not be going the way you want. You may not see the way ahead very clearly. You may have doubts about your ability to do what lies before you. You may wonder if you'll ever feel happy and whole again. You're in good company if you have such questions, for they're common to people in grief. But honest questions like these are not the final word. They are the first step on a path that leads elsewhere.

You can choose to have faith in your determination and your perseverance. You can choose to believe in your ability to learn as you go. You can choose to trust that there are others who want the best for you, that they are ready to stand with you when you need them. You can hold on to the belief that this time of difficulty can help strengthen you, that this time of loss can eventually help shape you for the better. In other words, you can choose to trust the process. It has worked for others. Now it can work for you.

■

# 12

## Build on this experience
## and use it for all it's worth.

Something has happened in your life that has presented a major obstacle, or perhaps several obstacles. Whatever you have lost, whatever has been taken from you, whatever you have left behind, keep this in mind: this unwanted experience is not just a stumbling block you must work your way around. It's also a building block you can put to use, if not now, then some time in the future. Here are eight suggestions for how you can do that:

■ *Remember it.* This is a significant period in your life. One reason this time has been so hard for you is that it's held such importance for you. This is not a time you can simply brush off or take lightly. So carry with you what this experience stands for. Perhaps it's a reminder of your ability to love, or to create, or to persevere. Perhaps it represents your better days, your better hopes, or your better self. Make it a part of you.

■ *Learn from it.* There's a lot of information available to you here. You can learn about yourself—your strengths, your priorities, your possibilities. You can learn about others too, and about how they respond to events like these. You can expand your knowledge about loss and grief and growth. In other words, you have the opportunity to learn about life itself, and about what's really important to you in life.

■ *Apply it to other situations.* The loss you have known is not your only loss. Something similar may happen again, and if it does, you will be better prepared. Something different may yet occur, and if it does, a part of this experience will carry over to that one. What you are learning now may even help you with your *previous* losses. You can re-visit those experiences and grieve them more completely as you come to understand them more fully.

■ *Validate your abilities.* By making your way through loss, you are accomplishing something really worthwhile. You are doing what's difficult, what may have seemed impossible. And as you're doing that, you're not just surviving—you're growing, even if you don't see it yet.

■ *Teach what you're learning.* What you're discovering can be of use to others. What you're learning the hard way is worth preserving and passing on. Even the simple telling of your story can serve to educate others.

■ *Reach out and help.* You can now say things to others that no one else can say, and in ways no one else can say them, because you're becoming a veteran. You understand. Your message and your example can offer a great deal to others— the permission to grieve, the possibility of healing, the promise of support, not to mention your offers of practical assistance.

■ *Deepen your sense of manhood.* What is happening to you affects you as a human being, but it also shapes you as a man. You can use this time to grow in how you deal with your emotions, how you relate to those close to you, how you open yourself to other people, men as well as women. You can look at those forces that have formed you as a male and determine which ones you want to affirm and which ones you want to modify, which you want to hang on to and which you want to leave behind.

■ *Live more fully.* Because of what you have been through, you can know in a new way the blessings of individual days, and individual lives, and this individual world. You can see life in all its richness, but you can do even more than see it—you can live it. This time of endings in your life can evolve into something more. It can become a time of new beginnings.

What is happening to you is too important to be ignored, too valuable to be left behind. Make it a part of who you've been and who you are. And allow it to influence who you're becoming: a deeper, richer person.

■

31

# In Summary

Keep these ideas in mind when you as a man consider your own grieving process:

- You will grieve in your own way, influenced by who you are, how you're made, what you've experienced, and how you've been raised.
- You're likely to seek a map to understand grief's terrain.
- You may use fewer words than those around you.
- You will be inclined to use your strength to connect with and heal your pain.
- You may choose to tap into your grief by taking action more than through interaction.
- You may place value on independence, quiet, and solitude as you grieve.
- You're likely to find meaning in caring for those around you as one aspect of your grieving process.
- You may wish to honor your loss through action that impacts the future more than talking about the past.
- You can use your courage to stand in the tension of grief.
- You can build on this experience and use it for your own growth.

Remember: there *is* a masculine style of grieving that deserves to be validated.

■

# A Man You Know
# Is Grieving

**James E. Miller** is a grief counselor, educator, and ordained minister who conducts workshops, leads retreats, and addresses conferences throughout North America, specializing in the areas of loss and grief, illness and caregiving, transition management, and spirituality. He has written, photographed, and published a total of sixteen books and seventeen videotapes. He hosts a website where his work can be previewed: *willowgreen.com*. Jim lives and works in Fort Wayne, Indiana. He and his wife Bernie are the parents of three children.

■

**Thomas R. Golden** LCSW is well known in the field of healing from loss. Tom's book *Swallowed by a Snake: The Gift of the Masculine Side of Healing* has been acclaimed by Elisabeth Kubler-Ross and others as a guide for understanding the masculine mode. Tom enjoys presenting workshops in the United States and Canada and is scheduled to tour Australia in 1999. His workshops are known to be entertaining and informative. Tom brings a gentle sense of humor and a gift for storytelling as he draws on his twenty years of practical, hands-on clinical experience. His work has been featured in *The New York Times, The Washington Post,* and *U.S. News and World Report,* as well as on CNN. For information on workshops Tom can be reached at his award winning website *webhealing.com* or by calling him at 1-301-670-1027.

■

# A Man You Know
# Is Grieving

## 12 Ideas for Helping Him Heal
## From Loss

James E. Miller
and
Thomas R. Golden

Willowgreen Publishing

*To Jordan and Chris, Whitten's sister and mother.*

We are indebted to a number of people who have assisted in various ways in the editing of this book. They include Michael Abrahams, Clare Barton, Chris Crawford, Darbie Golden, Miles Goldstein, Carrie Hackney, James Jones, John Ladd, Jennifer Levine, Bernie Miller, John Peterson, and Helen Wadsworth.

Willowgreen Publishing
PO Box 25180
Fort Wayne, Indiana 46825
219/424-7916

Library of Congress Catalogue
Card Number: 98-90047

ISBN 1-885933-27-4

You may have picked up this book for various reasons. Maybe you're the spouse or partner of a man who's suffered a loss and you want to learn all you can so you can be as helpful as possible. Maybe this man who's grieving is your father, your brother, your son, or some other close family member. Perhaps he's a friend or associate or colleague.

This man who's on your mind may have experienced the death of someone he's been very close to. That's the kind of loss most commonly associated with the word "grief." After a loved one dies, a man's life—*any* person's life—can be thrown into turmoil for an extended period of time. Yet grief is a natural response to many other kinds of losses as well. A separation or divorce leads to grief too. If his job has been terminated, or if he has made a significant career change, or if he has recently retired, grief will be one of the expected out-comes. The same applies if he has suffered an illness, injury, or disability that affects his day-to-day life, or if he has been handed a significant financial setback, or if he is undergoing a major life transition—a move to an unfamiliar place, for in-stance, or an upheaval in his family or personal life.

Grief comes as a result of any change that requires a person to give up or let go of what they have enjoyed or loved or found meaningful. The more disruptive that change and the larger the sense of loss they feel, the greater the grief they're likely to experience. People usually expect to grieve when a loved one dies. They may not expect that to happen with some of the other losses we've named. Consequently, it's possible for people to grieve without their being aware that's

5

what they're doing. That could be happening to the man you're concerned about.

Our culture doesn't make it easy for grieving individuals. Normally grief isn't talked about very much, and when it is, it's often discussed in whispers and with an air of discomfort. Often we don't know what to say to people who are grieving and therefore we may say nothing at all, which isolates such people even more than they already are. We have so few rituals to help people move through their sense of loss and to assist others—people like you—in honoring the grief that accompanies their loss.

This is the result: when we see people in grief, we may want to hurry them along so they can put it behind them as quickly as possible. That also puts it behind us too. And if we *don't* see signs of grief, even when such signs are to be expected, we may breathe a sigh of relief, because then we can act as if everything were normal. Only it's not.

There's another reason you may have picked up this book. You may be open to the idea of grief and you may understand its usefulness and importance, but you don't understand why it is that this man in your life is grieving the way he is. If the two of you are responding to the same loss, he may not appear as moved by it as you. He may talk about having to accept what cannot be changed. His grief may have a different speed than yours, a different intensity, a different rhythm. Just as you may not understand his ways, he may not understand yours.

One of our purposes in writing this book is to point out the various ways people can grieve. As the title indicates, we'll focus here on grief responses of men. But we want to be clear that we do not believe that men grieve only one way and women grieve another. As you'll read in the following pages, there are many variables and influences that affect how a particular person will respond to loss. In this book we'll be dealing with a masculine *style of grief*. It's important to keep in mind that it's not only men who grieve like this—some women do as well. And some men grieve in a way we commonly

associate with a more feminine style. These are not black-and-white categories. The way people grieve is more like a long continuum, with the more masculine style toward one end and the more feminine toward the other. Most of us are in the middle somewhere. But wherever we are on that line, around us are likely to be people of both genders.

We'll concentrate on one of those two genders, because that's what this book is about. We hope that what we've learned as men who have grieved and as professionals who work with grieving men will help you as you ponder what's happening with the man who's on your mind.

Jim Miller
Tom Golden

# 1

## Men are both born and raised
## to be the way they are.

It's no secret that men and women are different. These differences are sometimes obvious, sometimes not. While it's important not to stereotype either gender, it's equally important to understand that both men and women have their unique tendencies as to how they look, act, talk, think, and feel. Since this book is about men and grief, we'll focus on this half of the picture: how men are both genetically inclined and generally taught to behave in those ways we often regard as the more masculine.

■ *Males are already shaped at birth.* Some physical differences are part of a man's make-up from the moment he's born. For example, a man's brain tends to be designed a little differently than a woman's. The corpus callosum, that passageway which runs between the two halves of the brain, is often smaller in men and it may contain fewer neural connectors than a woman's brain. One theory is that this can limit how quickly and easily a man can process information back and forth between his brain's left and right hemispheres. That's especially important when it comes to grief, because one side of the brain specializes in processing emotions and the other side in processing thoughts. According to this theory, men may be at a physical disadvantage when it comes to having quick verbal access to the emotions. It takes them a little longer to do that.

Another physical difference relates to the hormone prolactin which is produced by the pituitary gland. Prolactin is instrumental in the formation of emotional tears—without a good supply of this hormone, it's more difficult to cry. While both sexes secrete a similar amount of prolactin at younger ages, males begin to produce significantly less once they've reached puberty. To a degree, many men are programmed by their bodies to cry less.

8

A third variable involves serotonin, a chemical produced by the human brain which influences people's moods. A deficit of serotonin can result in a number of problems, including depression. Recent studies have shown that men tend to produce serotonin faster than women. Consequently, for physical reasons alone men may be less susceptible to the heavy depression that sometimes accompanies grief.

■ *Males are shaped by the way they're raised.* Boys are much more likely than girls to be discouraged from crying when they're quite young. In fact, the expression of *many* emotions is likely to be dampened, both by what's said to boys and by the models they're given to follow—older boys and father figures, both in real life and in popular media. A few emotions are given more leeway in males, the most obvious being anger.

There are many other unique stresses young boys must experience, including the first separation from his mother when he's three or four years old. Suddenly he's no longer allowed in the bathroom with his mom. He's discouraged from touching his mother as he once did and as his sisters may still do. He is cut off at an early age from the source of his existence and he must find a way to adjust to this new reality.

Given these facts, how can you best relate to a man as he grapples with loss? You can enter this time with an open mind and an accepting attitude. Believe there are reasons he's acting the way he is and you'll be in a better position to understand those ways. Go into this experience with an inquiring spirit. What can you learn here? What does he have to teach you about his way of looking at the world? What might you learn together about the unique tendencies of the way you each grieve? His approach may be different from yours but that's all it is—different. It deserves confirmation.

■

# 2
## No two men respond to loss alike.

It's tempting to think in generalities: "All men behave one way and all women behave another." Various books, current cartoons, and popular wisdom encourage us to look upon life this way. As we've noted, there's evidence to suggest that men and women are created and shaped to have their differences. Yet another fact is just as true: however much a man is naturally different from a woman, he is also different from all other men. Every man is undeniably, unrepeatably unique.

■ *The man you're concerned about is unique because of his natural disposition.* Some men thrive on sports, whether it's playing, watching, or just talking about them. Other men couldn't care less. Some are mechanically inclined, while others can barely pound a nail. Something similar is at work when it comes to the way a man deals with loss. Some men approach their losses factually and intellectually, while others come at them more intuitively and emotionally. Some men have a lot to say; others speak very little. Some are comfortable discussing their grief. Others act as if the subject should never be broached.

■ *The man you're concerned about is unique because of what has happened to him in the past.* No one has led the same life he's led. No one else has known the identical combination of early influences and later experiences that have helped make him who he is today. One aspect of a man's uniqueness relates to the losses he's known before. He may have experienced many of them, making him a veteran. Or this may be an entirely new experience for him and he may be like a beginner, not knowing what to expect or what to do. If he's experienced significant other losses before, the feelings associated with those times may re-surface with this new loss.

■ *The man you're concerned about is unique because of the influences he's under today.* The kind of loss a man is grappling

10

with will influence how he responds, since some losses are more serious than others. It's likely that the death of one's spouse will stab more deeply than the death of a distant aunt or uncle. Being terminated from a job one has loved will probably require more time and energy to adjust to than leaving a job voluntarily when one is ready. Another influence is societal expectations. Some cultures permit a man to show his emotions openly, while other cultures expect him to act calm and appear stoic. Family expectations and self-expectations are also factors. So are the amount and kind of support a man receives during a time of loss. People who feel upheld by others tend to move more smoothly through their grief, and sometimes more quickly.

Each man, therefore, will enter grief in his own individual way. So what can you do as a person who cares?

You can expect him to be no other than who he is. He will probably respond as he's been raised to respond, and as he's comfortable responding. He may grieve like other men you know, or he may do it very differently. Believe that he is responding in the most authentic way he can, given who he is, what he has experienced, and how he has been influenced. Listen and respond to him without judgment. Avoid evaluating what he's doing or not doing.

Remember that every man has his own best ways, his own strengths, for moving into and through his grief. Whether he's inclined to be more solitary or to call upon others, whether he's likely to be slow and methodical or quick and energetic, support him in discovering and using his natural talents. You can help make a difference in the confidence he feels during a vulnerable time of his life.

■

# 3

## In our culture grief and manhood don't mix all that well.

Our culture has created an idealized image of what it means to be a man. He is strong and confident. First he thinks things through, then he forges ahead to do whatever the circumstances call for. He's cool and calm under pressure. Mostly, a man is independent—he relies not so much on others as on himself.

Through the years, two important human functions have helped define a man's relationships with others. He's a *protector*—he watches out for other people's safety and well-being. This applies especially to those he loves—spouses, partners, children, parents, close friends. It can also apply to others around him in his daily life. In addition, he's a *provider*—he takes care of other people's needs. He supplies food, clothing, and shelter for his family, as well as other amenities they require and deserve. He provides for needs other than physical ones, and sometimes for people other than his family.

When these masculine ideals and roles are internalized and taken as the norm, whether this is done by the man himself or by those around him, problems can occur. While there are many times in a man's life when such ideals and role expectations can present complications, one of the most obvious is when he finds himself in grief.

In many ways, grief asks the opposite of a man than what may be commonly expected of him. Grief has a will of its own, coming when and where it wants, leaving only when it's ready. Grief makes it hard for a man to appear cool and collected because it can sweep over him when he least expects it. It can diminish his ability to protect others if he's experiencing his own powerful emotions. He'll probably come to realize he cannot protect those he loves from their own experiences of loss and sadness. For those same reasons, he may not function

as well in his role as a provider. He may feel torn, thinking he ought to appear "strong," yet knowing that's not what's going on inside. In short, the cultural ideals of manhood may be in conflict with the realities of his personal grief.

One important way you can help a man who's dealing with a significant loss is to understand how our culture's ideals are guiding the way he lives his life, and especially the way it encourages him to deal with his grief. Try putting yourself in his shoes, if only partially, if only for a moment. Let him know that the ideals he's been handed are just that—ideals. They don't have to be lived up to. In fact, it's often better for everyone when they're *not*.

Another important way you can help a man who's grieving is to beware of trying too hard to help him. There are many things he can do only for himself. He must feel his own emotions. He must go through his own ups and downs as he adapts to his loss. He must learn from his own experiences as he moves forward in life. No matter how well-intentioned your motives, you ought not do for a man what is his alone to do.

Moreover, a man may resist being helped due to his inclination toward independence. He may associate "needing help" with "being weak," even if that's not the case. And whoever is on the receiving end of a helping gesture—whether it's a man or woman, an adult or child—can feel caught in an unequal relationship, with the helper somehow standing above the one who is being helped. Sometimes the helper needs to help more than the other person desires to be helped, causing distance rather than closeness.

Look closely at the reasons you do what you do in your helping role. Just as he's helpless to make everything right for everyone else, you're also helpless to make everything right for him. It may be hard for you to watch him grieve, but allowing his grief is one of the most beneficial things you can do. Remind yourself that when he's grieving, he's healing.

■

# 4

## A man who is grieving
## may not be very expressive about his emotions.

There are several reasons why a man may be less verbal about his feelings. If he takes his protector/provider roles seriously, he's likely to concentrate on the emotions of others. South African leader Nelson Mandela was very upset when his baby daughter died after a long period of around-the-clock care by his wife and himself. He said later of that time, "My wife was distraught, and the only thing that helped temper my own grief was trying to alleviate hers." The stance Mandela took in 1947 is the stance some men take today as they live out their protector roles.

Men sense the public display of their emotions can cause concern or discomfort for those who aren't used to seeing them act this way. "What does it mean that this person who represents such solid strength is so overcome?" some people may wonder. Men's pain has become a taboo in our culture. Many people don't want to see it, think about it, or talk about it. Consider, for example, how men are commonly portrayed on television—they work and engage in sports activities, they take stands and make jokes, they kill and get killed, and every once in a while they show a bit of awkward tenderness. But how often on television do you see a man in really deep emotional pain? There's only one place where a man's emotions are easily accepted in public: in the sports arena.

Many men have come to feel shame for shedding tears or showing emotional distress when others are around. A case in point is what happened to Edmund Muskie when he was the front-runner in the 1972 Democratic presidential primary. Speaking before TV cameras, he lashed out at a newspaper publisher for dishonest reports about Muskie's wife, Jane. As he did so, he started to weep in frustration and anger. Muskie was later to say of those few moments on camera, "That

14

changed people's minds about me. They were looking for a strong, steady man, and here I was, weak."

As we've already indicated, hormonal differences may influence how a man displays his emotions, and brain structure may help determine how quickly and easily he translates his feelings into words. Verbal expression of emotions is often simply not a man's forte or his interest. Studies indicate, for instance, that women on average speak quite a few more words a day than men do. So many men are not as practiced at putting words to emotions. It makes sense, then, that they would be less likely to connect their grief with their words.

What might all this mean for you, a person who wants to be attentive to a man who's grieving? It means, first of all, that you should not be surprised if his words are few or if he is slow to talk about what's going on inside. He may, in fact, say nothing at all. If there's silence, avoid rushing in to fill it up or cover it over. Perhaps you can join him in that quiet. Sometimes a look, a tear, or a touch may say more than words ever could, whether that's from him or from you.

If he chooses to speak, be an effective listener. Pay careful attention to what he says and how he says it. Don't interrupt with your questions or comments. Let him know you're with him by your visual and verbal cues, like nodding your head at times and saying "uh huh," "I see," and other short phrases that show your interest. Reflect back to him what you understand of his feelings when the time seems right, using your own words to get as close as possible to his meaning. If you learn your sense isn't quite accurate, ask him about what you missed and then try again. Validate his feelings and let him know they're normal and even healthy.

Remember that a lack of expression is not necessarily a lack of feelings. He can experience the same emotional intensity as someone who is more verbal with feelings. Never judge a man by the number of tears he sheds or the number of words he uses. His heartfelt expression may take other forms.

∎

# 5
## Men who are grieving often value their aloneness.

If you're the type who's inclined to talk about whatever is bothering or hurting you, it may be hard for you to understand that someone would prefer *not* to talk. And if you're one who turns naturally to other people for support when you're going through an upsetting time, you may wonder why other people would choose to go off by themselves. Yet it's true—some people seek solitude as their preferred way of grappling with life's losses.

Research supports what many of us already know: as a rule, men are more likely than women to place high value on their independence. Generally, men are more inclined to take pride in making their own way and in being self-reliant, whereas women are often inclined to look for relationship and interaction as they travel through life. In such a scenario, when a serious loss occurs, a man may tend to believe that the resulting grief is a burden that is his alone to bear. By this way of thinking, it would be unfair to expect others to shoulder it for him.

One of the authors once spoke with a man who told of being on a fishing expedition with three buddies when the Coast Guard brought him the tragic news his son had been killed in an accident. All four fishermen went back to shore, one of the friends drove this man to the bus station, and then he waited by himself all afternoon until he caught a bus for the six-hour ride home. As he told this story several years after that long, sad day, he still felt it was appropriate he had been left to return home unaccompanied. "The fishing was good," he said, "and this wasn't *their* problem—it was *mine*. I couldn't expect them to give up their trip just for that." Some men feel firmly that you shouldn't place on others what is yours alone to grapple with.

Some people find it more healing when they can surround themselves with quiet and solitude rather than conversation and company. These people may create short spells like this throughout the day, or they may go off by themselves for extended periods of time. One man goes alone regularly to his wife's grave so he can stand or sit for awhile as he quietly experiences his grief and soaks up the peacefulness he finds there. Another man takes a long, slow drive in his car and smokes his cigar. Another retreats to his garden and works for hours on end. Some men disappear into their woodworking shops with only the sound of their tools to keep them company. Others go backpacking in the wilderness. Whatever their methods, these men are simply trying to create a private healing space in which they can process, in the way that feels most natural, what is happening around and within them. As long as such activities serve to connect a man with his pain, then these times can be healing for him.

If this is how the man you know is choosing to do his grieving, you can support him in various ways. You can remember the reasons he may be doing what he's doing and place his actions in that context. You can accept that the choice he's making is the one that best suits him at that point in time, realizing that historically there's been a long and honorable tradition of people going off alone in order to facilitate their growth. At the same time, don't assume that you necessarily know when a man wants solitude or how much of it he wants. Speak with him about it. Ask him to give you some guidance so you won't be presuming or guessing each time.

In short, you can bless a man's journey as he goes in search of quietness and aloneness, if that's what he chooses. You can hold him in your awareness as he makes his way. Then you can greet him with warmth and love when he returns.

■

# 6

## Men often respond more cognitively to their loss.

One of the authors remembers viewing a local television newscast about a seven-year-old boy who had been killed near his home when a car suddenly went out of control. The TV crew interviewed the mother in her living room, surrounded by friends and neighbors, as she tearfully recalled her child's last day. Then the camera showed the father down the street where the accident occurred, pacing back and forth, trying to comprehend how the car could have gone out of control and killed his son in the way it did. The mother and father each found different ways to deal with their grief. She turned to the powerful resources of her relationships and her tears as she processed this experience in her search for meaning. He sought to bring some order to his chaos by turning first to his mental processes.

When a person responds cognitively to a loss, they're emphasizing thinking more than feeling, at least at that moment. They're trying to figure things out, consider things logically, and come up with an explanation or a plan that will help them deal with what has happened. Many men react this way, although certainly not all men do. Nor is it only men who deal with loss this way. But a larger percentage of men than women are more likely to choose this rational approach.

Many men are known to "keep a cool head" when something threatening happens. They've been trained that way by the examples of masculine behavior they've been given through the years. It also appears that their brains are wired to react in this way: "Respond first with thoughts, respond later with emotions."

Men sometimes take a problem-solving approach to their experience of loss. They first identify the trouble, then analyze it, then come up with a strategy to handle it. Finally they're ready to take concrete steps to solve the problem and rectify

18

the situation, as much as they're able. Men sometimes say they want to be "realistic" about what has happened so they can become clear about what they're to do from that point forward.

When men approach their grief by engaging in intellectual or work-related activities, it allows them to use their minds in a way they're accustomed. The man you know might be reading all he can about whatever he's facing, including reading about the toughest part of grief for anyone—the emotions. He might be studying grief and how it works, or learning about depression and how it appears. He might get involved in researching this topic that's hitting so close to home by attending a lecture, going to a library, or exploring the internet. Some men write their thoughts in journals or in letters. Others just keep track of everything in their heads, as they've done so many times before. However they choose to do it, these men use their thinking mode as a safe and natural way to begin connecting with their pain. It's a connection that can ultimately lead them toward their healing.

If the man you want to understand is responding cognitively to his loss, support him in doing what comes natural to him. Listen to his thoughts, his reasoning, his explanations. Pay attention to his findings. Maybe you can add to his knowledge in some way, if it seems appropriate, or join him in his search, if he asks you. He'll probably choose to respond in other ways too, either sooner or later. You can affirm the value of the various ways he chooses, realizing that the way he grieves today may not be the way he grieves tomorrow.

■

# 7

## Men often make active responses to their loss.

Perhaps the man you're thinking about has said something like this before: "You can't do anything about the past." It's an expression many men have been known to use. There's a second idea that usually accompanies it, whether it's spoken or not: "But you *can* do something about the future." Many men are drawn toward the future as a means of dealing with their loss. One of the more common ways they do this is by making an active, tangible, physical response.

■ *Some men respond actively with their practicality.* After Marc Klaas' daughter, Polly, was kidnapped and later found murdered, he devoted his energies toward the arrest and conviction of her killer. Once that was accomplished, he turned his attention to making sure her death was not in vain. He created the Klaas Foundation for Children which today teaches families and communities how to prevent crimes against children through personal action and legislative change.

After a popular 32-year-old man named Carter Seawall died of a heart attack in Charlotte, North Carolina, leaving behind a wife and two small children, his friends felt they wanted to honor him by *doing* something. Aware his older child had been helped by a non-profit agency that served the needs of grieving children, Carter's friends met with agency officials to ask what they needed. Learning of a wish to purchase an old $300,000 home for their headquarters, the friends went to work. The fund-raising video they created and the financial appeals they made all became a part of their healing process, and in just four months they had the entire amount in hand.

Men often look for practical, hands-on ways to respond to their losses. Depending on who they are, they may volunteer their services, donate or raise funds, build or repair things that help others, or raise people's consciousness about an issue related to their loss. They tie the action they take to the grief

they feel, believing that they can perhaps make a difference for those who are living and visibly honor the loss in some meaningful way.

■ *Some men respond actively with their creativity.* When Princess Diana died tragically in an auto accident, her friend and pop singer Elton John spent the next few days helping to write a song about her and then performed it at her funeral. "Candle in the Wind 1997" spoke not just for him but for many millions of people.

In 1986 Cleve Jones designed a three-foot-by-six-foot cloth panel to honor a friend who had died of AIDS. This was to become the first section of the AIDS memorial quilt, which by 1998 included over 42,000 panels, covered 18 acres, and beautifully represented the memories of hundreds of thousands of survivors.

Through the ages men have created drawings and paintings, done carvings and sculptures, written symphonies, performed music, composed poetry, and used about every medium imaginable to leave a record of their love, devotion, and sense of loss. Often these acts of creativity have not only helped these men heal, but they have also inspired others and encouraged their healing too. Senator George McGovern wrote a book in honor of his daughter Terry who died of an alcohol-related death. It was through the process of writing the book that McGovern grew in understanding his daughter and his grief. Now that it's published, the book can also help others in similar situations.

When you become aware that a man you know is engaging in an activity as a way of expressing his grief, respect it for what it is: a genuine grief response. What he does can be a form of talking without the words and even a form of crying without the tears. This method is just as valid as any other form of expression, and sometimes its eloquence is profound.

■

# 8
## Men respond to loss in spiritual ways.

Every person is a complete human being, made up of body, mind, heart, and soul. Therefore every man is capable of making a spiritual or soulful response to his loss.

■ *Some men turn to their religious faith.* A man may continue or increase his participation in religious observances. He may attend worship services, silent retreats, prayer meetings or study groups, bringing with him the thought of the loss he's experienced. He may carve out his own devotional times, read scripture, pray, or practice other disciplines. He may spend time one-on-one with a clergyperson or spiritual director, seeking to understand the ways of God, or to hear the call of God in his own life.

■ *Some men turn away from their religious faith.* Some men push away from it; others feel pushed away. The reasons can be many. They may find less meaning or satisfaction in their former practices when someone they love can no longer participate with them. They may feel lonely or estranged when they're surrounded by others, many of whom may not understand the depth of their loss. They may harbor disturbing questions regarding what they've been taught or what they've presumed about their faith. They may develop serious doubts. This turning away may be temporary, or it may last a long time.

■ *Some men make personal spiritual responses.* Whether or not a man has been a part of a worshipping community, he may seek soulful experiences or engage in spiritual routines which are independent of any one faith system. A common way this happens for men is through their connection with nature and the great outdoors. They may feel a sense of appreciation and awe as they witness the beauty of the natural world, as they watch the changing seasons, or as they wonder at the marvel of life itself. These experiences may come when they're engaged in an activity: standing in a stream fishing, for instance,

22

or photographing wildflowers in a field. Some men seek out places that speak to their present experience: deserts or mountains, rivers or oceans, windy beaches or dark forests.

■ *Some men respond spiritually by trying to discover meaning.* "Why did this happen?" a man might ask. "Why those I love? Why me? Why now?" In asking these and similar questions, he's attempting to make sense of what happened to him in the larger scheme of things. One man, realizing he had a terminal illness, wrote a small book about his life, ending it with all the important life lessons he had learned. Men who look for meaning after a serious loss are often preparing to answer fundamental questions: "What's really most important in my life?" "What can I do now that would add significance or value to what's occurred?" "How can I best live my life from this time onward?" Sometimes meaning emerges easily, appearing clear and sure. Other times it's slow and even painful in its coming.

If it appears that the man you know is ready to make a spiritual response, follow his lead. If he wants to talk, use the same kind of faith or spiritual language he uses. Remember that often the most sacred things are spoken in quite ordinary words. Similarly, some of the most meaningful and holy moments occur in very common and unexpected settings.

Support him in his own faith, if he speaks of one, rather than imposing yours on him. That is especially important if his loss is recent and raw. Give him room to bring up any doubts or uncomfortable feelings. Let him know that many people go through a dark night of the soul as they grieve if that happens to him.

Remember that his spirituality may express itself in unassuming ways. It may happen as he drinks a cup of coffee on the porch at sunrise, as he walks through a park in the rain, or as he sits silently holding a memento of his loss. He may not put many words to these times, but with your understanding, he won't have to.

■

# 9
## A man's grief usually unfolds in a natural way.

You cannot predict exactly how this man you know will grieve—what he'll do, when he'll do it, or for how long. There are too many variables, too many individualities that can influence what will happen. Be cautious, therefore, of any predictions that give precise, orderly stages and well-defined timelines to grief. That's not the way it works. Grief is much too unruly and far too personal for that. However, it's often possible to see an overall pattern to a person's grief if you look at it from a broad perspective.

If his loss has been sudden or devastating, he's likely to be in a state of shock for awhile. He may not believe whatever happened has really happened. As reality slowly sets in, so does the pain, often accompanied by many strong emotions. These feelings can be all jumbled up, making them seem confusing and conflicting. Sadness, anxiety, irritability, anger, fear, guilt, shame, and helplessness are all commonplace. You may see these feelings displayed, and then again, you may not. He may act scattered and distant, or appear insecure and a bit off balance.

As time passes, he's likely to begin slowly and gradually negotiating the changes that are necessary in order to move through his grief. He may seem depressed and lacking drive and energy, wondering if he'll ever feel much better. This can go on for some time. But in time he usually starts to find small things that give him hope and bring him joy, just a few at first, and then more. Little by little he senses re-awakening potential. He can still feel sad and upset periodically, but as time goes along, and as he devotes himself more and more to the possibilities, a fullness of life gradually returns to him and he becomes more accepting of what has happened.

If his loss has been the death of a loved one, he doesn't necessarily say a final goodbye as a way of completing his grief,

24

but he finds a way to carry that person within him as he moves on through life. Whatever the nature of his loss, his journey through grief will not lead him back to being the same person he was before. Chances are he'll be different; he'll be changed by his experience. In the best of situations, with equal amounts of proper support, hard work, and persistence, he'll be changed for the better.

What usually helps a man early in his grief is for a person like you to simply be present and to let him know you care by what you do as much as by your words. Let him talk as much or as little as he desires. Allow him to repeat himself if he wants. If he wonders, let him know it's common for grieving people to feel they're going a little crazy occasionally. Tell him that feeling a little crazy is a good sign you're normal.

Hang in with him during any long, depressing periods he may go through. Don't force cheerfulness upon him—just be yourself and let him know you appreciate his company, whatever he's feeling. Maintain contact with him. Keep inviting him into your life and don't be offended if he's slow to take you up on your offers. Trust his sense of what's right for him, then ask him again another time. Don't desert him.

When it seems appropriate, offer your perspective about the changes and the progress you see with his grief, his growth, and his life. Celebrate with him any joys and victories. Discuss with him, when he's ready, any lessons he's learned, any hopes he's harboring. For those times when it's hard for him to hope, try this: tell him you'll hold his hope for him until he's able to do it himself. Make his continued growth a part of your wishes or prayers, even when you're apart. It can make a difference.

■

# 10

## Men can use their experience of loss to claim their wholeness.

After a man loses something that's been a crucial part of his life—a critical relationship, his job, his home, his health, his security—he often feels less than whole. Some men describe this as being torn apart or thrown into turmoil. There's a paradox at work here. When men find the courage to experience their grief in its fullness, to enter the chaos of the loss a bit at a time, they offer themselves the opportunity to heal and move toward wholeness.

■ *The man you know can use his experience of grief to seek the fullness of life.* The word *heal* comes from the same word which means *whole*. To heal, therefore, means to find or return to your sense of wholeness. A man may not realize this is happening to him while he's in the midst of it, of course, but he can facilitate his own healing by doing what comes natural to him. Should he be one who cries with grief, each shedding of tears will help release the tension and sadness he feels and serve as a step forward. Should he be one who uses his actions as a way to grieve, each activity he associates with his loss will be a part of his return to life. The same goes for any related reading or study he does, any thoughts or feelings about his loss he communicates, any assistance or protection he provides others who are also grieving. The secret is to associate whatever he does with his own loss.

■ *The man you know may take this present experience of loss as an opportunity to heal from other such experiences.* Any serious loss brings up secondary losses which need to be grieved as well. If his mate dies or he divorces, he will lose more than just that relationship. Other losses might include his home, his network of coupled friends, his financial security, and his accustomed family life, to name just a few examples. Something similar happens if his job ends or his health fails—those losses

ripple out, creating others. Every such loss requires the man's conscious attention and its own grief response.

Something else may come into play—previous losses which are unrelated to this experience, ones he is not yet at peace with. Perhaps an important person died or otherwise left his life when he was younger. If he has not yet acclimated himself to what happened, the feelings from that earlier time may visit him again, seeking a greater sense of resolution. That will help him in the long run. But in the short term he will have more to deal with than just what happened recently. He may experience more unrest and turmoil for awhile.

■ *The man you know can use this time to claim his wholeness as a human being.* Grief often throws men into emotional states that are foreign ground for them. This foreign ground can be painful and treacherous, but this very treachery offers a man a glimpse into his depths—depths he may rarely have experienced. There is an opportunity in disguise here. Through experiencing the powerful emotional chaos of grief, individuals can own their vulnerability in a new way. Through standing in the tension of the grief, they may find their softer sides. Through their courage to withstand the intensity of their turmoil, they can become more sensitive to the pain of others.

You can show your acceptance of these various facets of a man's grief as they show themselves, letting him know that you appreciate what he's going through and you respect him for the way he's going through it. You can affirm his human dimensions. You can show your own humanness. There's one thing more you can do which will help as much as anything else. To learn about it, turn the page.

■

# 11

## A good way to help a man heal is to concentrate on your own healing.

It hurts to see someone you care about when they're in deep grief. It can hurt even more if this person is a man you know whom you've seldom or never seen this way. If you're like many people, you may wish you could take his pain away so he won't be as upset or feel as sad as he does. You may be tempted to do all you can to make this time go faster for him or to make this experience easier for him. Those are common reactions. But one of the best ways you can care for a man who's grieving is to focus not only on his healing but also on your own.

If the loss he's facing also impacts you, then you must be sure to deal with your own feelings and responses. Just as he must do his own grieving, so must you. Your grief will probably show itself differently. It will have its own intensity and its own fluctuations which will not exactly mirror his. Keep in mind that when you, as a grieving person, do for yourself what you alone can do, you encourage him to do the same for himself.

You may be experiencing a current loss which is unrelated to his, or you may be dealing anew with a loss which occurred some time ago. You may be unaffected by loss yourself but feel somewhat anxious about the changes you see in this man as he grieves. Another possibility is that you're feeling just fine and quite comfortable with your role. Whatever is happening, it's important you take responsibility for yourself. But it's not only important to you—it's also beneficial to him. He may be a man who doesn't like to have his feelings put in the spotlight. He may wish to guard his privacy or protect his quietness. By being aware of what's happening to him, and by taking your cues from him, you can help create an atmosphere in which he will feel more free to work through his grief in the ways that suit him best.

28

Surely you've been in the company of people who've acted very tense or angry, unrelated to anything you've said or done. It doesn't feel very comfortable, does it? Sometimes it's hard to be yourself in situations like that. Here's another example: maybe someone in your family was once seriously ill for a long period of time. You learned the hard way that such an illness affects the entire family, even though it's only one person who's sick. Something similar can happen in reverse. When you're around someone who's healthy and whole, it's easier for you to be that way too. When others around you are conscious of promoting their own healing, there's an energy in the air that encourages you to do the same thing. That's the sort of influence you can bring to this situation.

In addition to offering loving attention to the man you care about, use this as an occasion to continue your own development as a maturing human being too. By doing this, the two of you will enter into this time as equals. You'll be able to learn with one another and from one another. Together you'll be able to create an environment that's conducive to growth for *both* of you.

■

# 12
## A masculine style of grieving is as valid as any other.

Through the years you've developed your ideas about what's to be expected when people grieve. These notions are reinforced by the way grief is depicted on television and in movies and how it's written about in articles and books. Your ideas also come from what you've been told by others through the years, as well as how you yourself have grieved in the past and how friends and family members grieve yet today.

Most grief professionals encourage bereaved people to talk about what's happening around them and what's going on inside them. The wisdom of this "talk therapy" is taken for granted. Then along comes someone, perhaps someone you know, who does it a different way—they're less inclined to put everything into words and more inclined to take a quieter approach. Talking, at least about personal matters, may not be their medium.

There's an idea that people in grief are likely to cry and express sorrow and display other emotions. Then along comes someone who cries little or not at all, someone who deals with their loss more intellectually and philosophically. Such people are not necessarily denying their grief—they're just responding in their own way.

Many people can't imagine making their way through a time of grief without gathering a network of friends and supporters around them. There are some, however, who seem to prefer a different way. It's not that they're friendless—it's just that they value their privacy and solitude.

While many people report that it's hard to concentrate on other matters when they're grieving and they don't have the energy to do much at all, some people throw themselves into a form of work or some other activity for extended periods. When they somehow connect the activity they're engaged in

with their loss, they're finding ways to do their grieving too.

Our thesis is that both ways of healing—the more masculine style and the more feminine style—are valid. Whether the person who's grieving is a man or a woman, each person will have his or her own natural ways of dealing with loss. Just because some of those ways are less visible to the eye, less noticeable to the ear, or less apparent to the mind does not make them any less genuine. The secret for every grieving individual is to use whatever is their natural expression as a way to lead them into their grief, so they can chip away at it, little by little.

However grief works itself out in individual lives, it is a remarkable process. At sad, even heart-breaking times of people's lives, it leads them from the security of what-used-to-be toward the possibility of what-can-yet-be. Grief doesn't cover up and smooth over what happened. Grief exposes it to the light so it can be dealt with and worked through, as much and as fully as possible. Grief doesn't lead a person back to their former life. It leads them forward to new or renewed life. It doesn't patch things together; it helps bring healing. Grief doesn't fill up the holes; it leads to greater wholeness. That's true for the man you know, and it's just as true for you.

■

# In Summary

Keep these ideas in mind when a man you know is grieving:

- Our culture discourages men from openly emoting.
- At the same time men have been judged for *not emoting* and therefore may find themselves in a double bind.
- A man has physical differences which can impact his way of healing.
- A man's way of healing may be less visible and more subtle.
- A man's grief is often connected more with the future than with the past.
- Just because a man is more silent does not mean he isn't grieving.
- Every man is unique in the way he approaches his own healing.
- A man's healing can be influenced by his tendency toward independence.
- Men may prefer time alone in order to heal.
- Men may respond to their loss more cognitively.
- A man is likely to find ways to connect with the pain he feels with an action he can take.

Remember: there *is* a masculine style of grieving that deserves to be validated.

■